An Epistle
to the Moderately Miserable

Titles in the Series

Letters to the Devoted Follower of Christ

(in the order in which they were written)

AN EPISTLE TO THE MISERABLE
AN EPISTLE TO THE MODERATELY MISERABLE
AN EPISTLE ON JUDGMENT

An Epistle

to the

Moderately Miserable

By

A Little Anchor of the Church

Scriptures quoted from the King James Version (KJV) of the Bible. Please note that pronouns referring to God have been capitalized, though they are not in the KJV Bible.

The Little Anchor logo is derived from an image in the public domain and it and the name Little Anchor Books have no association with any other publishing company, nor was it intended they do so. By request, this volume has been self-published.

ISBN-13: 979-8-3304-0420-9

AN EPISTLE
TO THE
MODERATELY MISERABLE

My dear friend in Christ —
Your reply to my brief epistle expressing my sympathy regarding your state of misery reached me.[*] I was very glad to hear that my initial letter helped you in some way. I would be glad

---

[*] Please see the little book *An Epistle to the Miserable.*

to share more on the subject of the spiritual as long as you are willing to receive my modest offerings. I am very glad to put my words in epistle form so that you may read them or not as the Holy Spirit leads you to do.

I must say that it was not at all my intent to offend you. By declaring that you felt miserable by the state of things was only what I perceived to be the truth. But it is the lot of the soul to declare truth to the self that it does not otherwise wish to receive from others. That is, we may be perfectly able to tell our self we are miserable, but we do not much appreciate others saying the same to us. I understand. Perhaps you feel I ought to ask forgiveness from you, but I say that I take no offense at your offense, but I cannot rightly apologize when I made a sincere effort to give you God's truth as it was revealed to me.

You tell me you are not really miserable, that you are relatively happy in your unpaid, without recompense, and extremely tiring service to the Lord and those around you, as though a good Christian ought to be, as though this attitude is the Christ-follower's badge of honor. My friend, I say unto you in Jesus' Name, understanding the condition in which you have been for so long: grace and peace be unto you from God our Father and Jesus His One and Only Son; and may the fellowship of the Holy Spirit be with you every moment.

Let us begin, then, by stating that while you have remained

faithful to the calling the Lord placed on you, you have been feeling of late moderately miserable—worn down by many pressing duties; worn thin by countless interruptions that seem peripheral to your personal calling as a devoted follower of Christ; and just in general worn out by constant assailing from that unholy triumvirate, the world, the flesh, and the devil. Can we agree on this? I believe we can (though I hear your agreement offered in a mildly begrudging tone, which I can also fully understand, having experienced the same many times in myself). So let us continue.

It is no sin to feel miserable, and it is useless to deny that life is not always happy, though it is very important we endeavor to speak over ourselves and others edifying words of faith rather than negative prognostications. We can always say that God is constantly faithful, always good, never mistaken, and is ceaselessly laboring toward our success in life within the boundaries of His good will for us. Confess to Him your misery, but also find one thing for which you can give Him thanks. Sometimes this is all He wants or expects to hear from us when the soul feels depressed. Regardless that you need to be honest with God, do not leave out whatever gratitude you can render.

It also would not hurt to utter a few prayers for those you know to be in need in some way. It may not make you feel much better, but God is able to do more for others and for us when we declare His good intent toward His creation. And He will take your prayers and use them as seeds toward a harvest of greater faith in your soul. I realize it is challenging to persevere while the crops are growing—the soul grows impatient to store up the goodness being brought forth by its labor—but creation is of *His* design, and seedtime and harvest is His abiding principle for us.[*]

From my vantage point, you have done no wrong, such as that which is at times the cause of our misery (for I wondered if you questioned whether some sin had

---

[*] Genesis 8:22—"While the earth remaineth, seedtime and harvest, and cold and heat, and summer and winter, and day and night shall not cease."

provoked it)—no more so any-
way than those weaknesses every
person struggles with, such as
being easily distracted or the
nagging sense that your self-
discipline ought to be much
greater than it is after all this
time. This is normal. Do not con-
clude that God measures you by
the same rod you use on yourself.
He looks for overall consistency,
the exercise of virtues that
eventually results in growth. He
is wholly unintimidated by
whether the plant of your soul
grows so many spiritual microns
each day.

As children have growing
spurts, so does the soul progress
this way. It is pointless to be
fixated on what you feel is not
happening in your soul. And it is
a waste of energy wondering

whether you have by your own sin brought such misery upon yourself. When we keep our soul surrendered to God and trust Him with our care, He will be faithful to His fatherly covenant to us and will cause His Holy Spirit to convict us of any real sin. If you are not feeling such conviction, do your best to keep renouncing the misery — that quiet stance of soul that inwardly declares, "I refuse to speak with you on this subject. God says I am well in hand, and so there is nothing more to say." And if you are feeling such conviction, let the misery express itself in humility before God. Plead the Blood of Jesus and bow before Him, face to ground. He will set things right for you, and then you will endeavor to avoid the sin that brought you to this miserable state.

Do you recall what it was like as a child? It felt like nothing special was happening in us while we observed many things occurring for others. Then, one day at the end of a long, warm, active summer, someone we had not seen since the beginning of that season told us how much we had grown. Did you feel yourself growing? No, of course not. You went on with your activities and let your body take care of itself. You just fed, watered, exercised, and rested it. But all the while God made it grow.

Spiritually much the same is occurring in the soul at any given time in the person intent on growing in God. Is it not written, "And He said, So is the kingdom of God, as if a man should cast seed into the ground; and should sleep, and rise night and day, and the seed should spring and grow up, he knoweth not how"?* And the Book also teaches us that "neither is he that planteth any thing, neither he that watereth; but God that giveth the increase."†

We are indeed responsible for feeding our soul with heavenly manna—Christ, our Bread of Life—but God is responsible for raining the manna down around us.‡ We are expected to bring

---

* Mark 4:26-27
† I Corinthians 3:7
‡ John 6:48-51—"I am that bread of life. Your fathers did eat manna in the wilderness, and are dead. This is the bread which cometh down from heaven, that a man may eat thereof, and not die. I am the living bread which came down from heaven." See Exodus 16 regarding

ourself for our refreshment to the deep well of the clean, sparkling waters of Heaven, the Living Waters of Christ's abiding presence.* We are also expected to exercise our soul with the kind of moderate movement that keeps one limber and healthy; this is the exercise of our faith—that we believe God is† and that His word to us on anything is good.‡

---

manna: "Then said the LORD unto Moses, Behold, I will rain bread from heaven for you" (v. 4).
* John 7:37-38—"Jesus stood and cried, saying, If any man thirst, let him come unto Me, and drink. He that believeth on Me, as the scripture hath said, out of his belly shall flow rivers of living water." He was making application of Isaiah 12:3— "Therefore with joy shall ye draw water out of the wells of salvation."
† Hebrews 11:6—"…he that cometh to God must believe that He is…"
‡ Proverbs 30:5—"Every word of God is pure." [I.e., without imperfection] And Jesus Himself testified that "Thy word is truth" (John 17:17).

And lastly, we are ordered to take adequate rest when weary.* These are our responsibilities as living, developing spiritual entities just as a growing child occupies itself with the same in the natural realm. And the natural was intended to teach us of the spiritual.†

(I speak to you as one devoted to following Christ, and so I say to you things I would not say to just any believer. Only the most

---

* Matthew 11:28—"Come unto Me, all ye that labour and are heavy laden, and I will give you rest." Notice that despite the graciousness of the statement, He is still issuing a command, and divine commands are to be obeyed.
† Colossians 2:17—[These are that] "which are a shadow of things to come; but the body is of Christ." That is, outward matters are the type and shadow of the real substance of things, which is the spiritual reality in God. The author of Hebrews teaches the same; see Hebrews 7-10.

devoted will exercise their faith as the athlete in preparation for great games. Of the masses God is satisfied with the marginal efforts they make. So be careful you don't judge a soul by its lack of greater devotion because God may not be requiring that soul to render it. That it is kept in a state of salvation might be His higher priority—for some would reject God if true evil were revealed to them, believing its presence beside us is the equivalent of God having wronged those who were affected by the evil. It is far better that such souls be brought home to Heaven, if that is what it must come to, than that they remain on earth only to renounce their faith. You be faithful to your calling, even if it seems the Lord is requiring more of you than of others, and leave them to God.)

Do not make this more complicated than it needs to be. You are a child to God, and He expects of you only what He expects of all children. Certainly each one has odd chores (or it ought to, or it struggles later to comprehend why it should in some way serve others rather than the world being there to serve itself — which is only to be expected in one of the world, but not in one who professes to be reborn in Christ, who is the humblest Servant of God), but there is also time for rest and play.

We think too much of our leisure, and planning big expeditions for relaxation fails to make much sense to me — though

I am by no means saying that all must live in the degree of seclusion that my calling has required of me. If one needs to escape for a brief period a home or community filled with people and noise and tries to reach a quiet place, this pleases God very much. But to journey to a distant tourist area when vacation is needed—to surround oneself with activity and throngs of people and ceaseless noise—well, one may return having had some fun, but I would take a chance on saying that the spirit is not strengthened an iota. Only the fleshly part of the soul is fed at such times. That it *feels* good is the biggest indicator of which part of oneself is being energized. Take such trips as part of the life-blessing God has bestowed on you if you wish to do so. But don't pretend that kind of vacation is the solution your soul needs at times like this. It does not need soul-relaxation. It needs spiritual renewal and rest. The first can be had by almost any leisurely recreation that appeals to you, and take recreation as you are inclined to do. Surrender yourself to the leading of the Holy Spirit for keeping a check on your recreation times. He will nudge you if you are indulging yourself too much or too often when God would have you be about something more profitable. Spiritual renewal can only be had through the soul's surrender to divinely ordained means of refreshment—for instance, the solitude and silence that invites the presence of God.

In general, misery of whatever degree is relieved by one thing: rest in Jesus Christ our Lord. The soul needs consciously reminded now and again that God loves it with a love that is strong as death* and that its responsibilities do not extend further than the responsibilities of a soul under the protection of its guardian. That is, pursue your activities as you believe are your responsibility, but leave it to your Protector to sound the alarm if something is wrong. Do you question this care? Do you wonder if this implicit trust is the answer to all the myriad annoyances that all together have caused this state of misery? Do you think your misery will be

---

* Song of Solomon 8:6

relieved by encountering God in the kind of by-the-way encounter between you and an acquaintance you meet on the street? We so often feel rushed by the duties of the day to get moving, and I realize it can be very difficult to submit oneself to rest before activity, but this is the principle: rest then activity, stillness then movement.*

Hear then the word of the Lord: "Many waters cannot quench love, neither can the floods drown it: if a man would give all the substance of his house for love, it would utterly be contemned."† This is the quality and degree of Love which cares for you night and day. Yes, we

---

* Genesis 1:5—"And the evening and the morning were the first day."
† Song of Solomon 8:7

are expected to grow up into mature spiritual men, as I stated in my previous letter. And it is written, "But speaking the truth in love, may grow up into Him in all things, which is the head, even Christ."* Yet in contrast to God, the highest developed souls are still as little children. Does any of this comfort you at all?

An outward manifestation of the immediate transformation of your feelings is not necessary. Not seeing or feeling change is not the equivalent of nothing having changed. Something is always occurring in the soil of the soul, whether of health or harm. To remain as we are is to en-

---

* Ephesians 4:15. And I Corinthians 14:20 says, "Brethren, be not children in understanding: howbeit in malice be ye children, but in understanding be men."

courage stagnation. So do not examine your feelings as the decisive word of whether your misery has improved. It is unnecessary, and it is often counterproductive because it places too much emphasis on feeling.

Remember the two mountains: the two mountains between which the soul must choose to make its life: either on the mount of faith or the mount of feeling. God gives us clearly defined choices. It is good or evil, darkness or light, sinfulness or righteousness, etc. And it is either faith or feeling. Try to feel some relief that He does His best to boil things down for us so that we can easily see the contrast between choices. The grey areas will remain as long as we dwell in a land where the sun rises and sets;

they do not exist in a Place where the Light ever shines. But as we grow, God clarifies our vision so that we can better discern lines of demarcation. Sussing out the good choice becomes much easier as we journey along the Way of Salvation. (Yet do not ever consider that you know all you need to know to get by. Continue to seek after Truth.)

That matters of feeling are mixed up in the life of faith is a given. The person of faith does not aspire to be without feeling. Jesus never worked toward such a state, so as our Example, neither should we.* It is the abiding principle, the energizing force by

---

* I Peter 2:21—"For even hereunto were ye called: because Christ also suffered for us, leaving us an example, that ye should follow His steps."

which one lives, that is the question. Will the soul live preponderantly influenced by feeling or by faith? This is every soul's choice whether it consciously realizes it or not. You can at least thank God for your sense of misery if it has brought you to a greater understanding of or commitment to your faith.

Some would argue that there is also the valley of fact which lies between the two mountains and that this is where they are determined to live. And while in a sense this is not wrong — for our fact as believers is the Word of God and what it declares we are to take as true — abiding there constantly has its own problems. I would dare to say that souls who have invested much in property in the valley of fact are vulnerable to flooding and rockslides. From the mountain of feeling can come unexpected flash floods whose sudden force has the power to wipe out in a moment everything we have built over many years; and from the mountain of faith can come the massive Boulder, that Rock which is Christ. It can come rolling into the soul's path in season and out, for It is on a mission that is greater than any single person. God desires our ability to hear His voice so that we will heed His direction to *get out of the way* when the Rock comes rolling by. Illustrating this would require a separate letter. Suffice it to say, this is the only rock in existence that moves of its own volition,* and those who do not stumble on It (as all will from time to time because It is far larger than we will ever be†), are crushed beneath Its oncoming force.

Part of our misery often comes from believing we are more than we are. We do not want to get out of the way because this can feel slighting to the soul. It has its plans and purposes, and it tends

---

* I Corinthians 10:4—"And did all drink the same spiritual drink: for they drank of that spiritual Rock that followed them: and that Rock was Christ."
† Consider Romans 9:32-33—"Because they sought it not by faith, but as it were by the works of the law. For they stumbled at that stumblingstone; as it is written, Behold I lay in Sion a stumblingstone and rock of offence: and whosoever believeth on Him shall not be ashamed." Matthew 21:44—"And whosoever shall fall on this stone shall be broken: but on whomsoever it shall fall, it will grind him to powder." See also I Peter 2:8.

to want to remain in the center of things; it does not naturally gravitate toward the sidelines. So it gets run over by the Rock whose mission may not require at that time its seemingly big name or exalted talents, and indeed it is in the way of the path on which that Rock is moving at building speed. If we think the will of God at work for many will come to a grinding halt for us simply because we refuse to get out of Its way for the sake of our own purposes, I believe we are in error. We tend to suffer divinely occurring wounds at such times (though not divinely inflicted ones according to His will, which would have preferred we get out of the way).* The more you can surrender your sense of self to Christ, the more your misery will lessen.

So do not be too hard on yourself. These are lessons we all have to learn. It is the rare soul who has so little self-will that the Way of Christ is easy for it. And even those self-effacing souls who live

---

* For instance, a pastor of a large church senses the movement of the Holy Spirit trying to work in his services, or he has some of his congregation telling him this is so, yet he refuses to deviate from the firm template for the weekly service. If God intends that this occur (rather than that He withdraw the manifestation of His Spirit from there), this pastor may suffer substantially in influence (or ego) because he would not get out of the way. It would not be at all improbable that his congregation would want to replace him after this movement for a shepherd who will permit a freer rein.

to please others are not as selfless as might appear: they are often putting the desires of their fellow souls above those of God. Jesus never said following Him would be easy; He assured us however that in doing so we would find eternal life.* But do not put so much emphasis either on the self-sacrificing devotion of a true follower that you somehow reason yourself out of the truth that God "is able to do exceeding abundantly above all that we ask or think, according to the power that worketh in us."† In short, be diligent also to receive the good things He is always wanting to give you, such as adequate rest after labor, nourishment after

---

* John 12:50—"I know that His command leads to eternal life."
† Ephesians 3:20

fasting, and prosperity after sacrificial generosity.

If you believed by my former letter that I was making light of your misery merely because I encouraged you to exercise faith in response to it, you mistook my meaning. I say again to lessen the risk of being misunderstood, to feel or to be miserable is no light matter — to the soul or to God. We are too content to remain in it, and God knows it is best to have it dispelled as soon as possible. So while we feel so miserable we cannot bear being cheered (for encouragement feels belittling to our great misery), God would have us be cheered. It is a corner hard to get out of, I freely admit. And because of this, it should not be taken lightly. If I had, I would have only replied with a superficial note declaring you to cheer up, this too will pass. Yes, this too will pass, but not always without some exercise of faith on our part.

Yes, your best recourse is rest, spiritual rest to be sure, but most of us cannot seem to grasp hold of spiritual rest without also availing ourself of some physical rest. Perhaps this is why the Lord kept the custom of the Sabbath* — because as our Example, He showed us what would be beneficial for us, "for He knew what was in man."† The weekly day of rest was given to remind us that

---

* Luke 4:16—"And He came to Nazareth, where He had been brought up: and, as His custom was, He went into the synagogue on the sabbath day, and stood up for to read."
† John 2:25

God is our salvation; we do not save ourselves by our labors.*

In every way He showed us how to live, He understood what life here was like for us — our tendencies toward loose living, our unspiritual mindsets, our focus on the unnecessary mundane, etc. — and He knew how we would need to live in order to get by, to grow, and to thrive. The more the soul adheres to His Example, the better its soil for seeds and their harvests — for planting and for expected ends. So as difficult as it can be to let oneself be cheered, it is necessary for the overcoming of one's faith. It is especially vital in these days that we form a habit of response — feeling followed by faith. We

---

* Deuteronomy 5:12-15

certainly do feel negative emotions, but then as professing believers we respond by the exercise of faith. It is not the feeling of them that might be counted as sin but what we choose to do in response.

For a long time the Body of Christ got by on its feeling — good feeling for God, sympathetic feeling for the lost and abused, indignant feeling for consciously committed evils, and so forth. And feeling is not wrong in itself. It is just not higher than faith, nor is it its equal. Now great trials have come, and this feeling is insufficient to see the soul through to the end.

Only in God, the Perfect and Pure One, can feeling equal faith because there are no impurities in His feelings to corrupt His faith.

And God does also possess faith. This is why He has a right to ask it of us. His faith is firstly in Himself: He never doubts He can accomplish what He promises He will do. His faith is also in His Son — this part of Himself He sent out from Heaven and incarnated in human form.* Living as Man for a time caused Him to ex-perience the temptations of Man. That He never succumbed to these temptations does not necessarily mean they were not felt by Him. And He also underwent His own Temptation which targeted those areas in which weaknesses might be found that God-as-Man might manifest. What might He be tempted to do with such a life, the Essence of God filling His earthly

---

* Philippians 2:5-11

32

vessel? It would be like Galadriel's mettle being tested at arm's length by the Ring of Power.* God the Father had to exercise faith that His Son would be faithful to His calling as defined by the Father throughout many attempts to distract, to deceive, and to destroy Him throughout His life. And every time the Holy Spirit is sent out to operate in this earth, God has faith that this Spirit will conduct Himself in complete accord with the will of God, that He will not deviate from the unity of the Trinity.

Many persons seem to believe, whether intentionally or not, that God places on us a standard of

---

* See chapter 7 of *The Fellowship of the Ring* by J.R.R. Tolkien.

behavior He fails to appreciate is extremely difficult for us to live up to. They believe He cannot comprehend just how hard it is not to wallow in our dejection, how hard it is to pull our self out of its doldrums. The truth of the matter is just the opposite really: God understands exactly how hard it all is for us, and that is why it feels like He is hard on us, because He knows He can't give us an easy way out if the easy way is not really a way back to the Path of the Christ-life.

That He never gave into the temptations to self-pity and misery is not at all the same as saying He never stood near enough to them to appreciate what we are going through. Yet He knows that if we do not train and prepare, we will not make it.

We will stumble and fall along the way; the Rock will bowl over us; the floodwaters of life's greatest troubles will drown all semblance of that devoted walk with Christ. And see too how some never leave Egypt. They did not leave and wish to go back, as some of those did after the Red Sea experience*: they never had the courage to leave it in the first place. By faith in God's promises of a better life, you left Egypt. That is, you left it for a life filled with less self and more divinely chosen blessings — rather than the ones we choose for ourselves. Don't let the enemy steal away what you have gained. Look back at how very far you have come

---

* E.g., Exodus 16; Exodus 17; Exodus 32; Numbers 14...

before you decide to give up —
not that you are consciously
contemplating doing so, I am
sure; but having been where you
are, I know the enemy takes the
opportunity to suggest such
things to us.

Remember that it is like an
athlete training for the Olympics
or some other highly special com-
petition. Would you expect the
athletes to achieve places of
competing at those events if they
had not undergone rigorous
training? Or a mountain climber
trying to scale one of the tallest
mountains in the world, or a
spelunker aspiring to descend
deeper into earth's abyss than
any other has before? Their very
lives are at risk without proper
training. If they fail or fall, it is
very possible they won't be

coming back. And if we really knew the true heights and depths of our faith, as persons who are still aspiring to discover about our earth (believing present knowledge has failed to reveal all), we would be instilled with the proper fear of God when He tells us to attend to His voice.

Athletic training is required for souls who aspire to true faith. Without rigorous training, our faith either cannot compete in the greater games, or its life is even at risk depending on what feat it must perform in order to return home, home being that place of continuous habitation in God. And it is a mistake to believe we already know God's vast heights and depths.

Misery is no insubstantial issue, its molecules dispersed

with a wave of the hand. And what the soul must do to move out of such a state, even simply to pass beyond the feeling of it, is not some little effort — at least not in the beginning. With enough practice, getting back up again can become a natural response. But the soul cannot scale to the heights of Heaven if the only exercise it gets is an occasional stroll in the garden of God. And even with rigorous training, it still feels the pull upon its muscles when it competes in the greater games. Everyday exercise has become easy to the well-trained soul, but the games themselves require such a high level of performance that it is still challenged by them. So do not be surprised when your faith is challenged, as though you had expected to move beyond such testing. We must all continue to take up our cross.* –which is the daily training that enables us to be eligible to compete in the greater games of faith.

Do not let the misery overcome you. You are stronger than you realize. It is the weak of faith who cannot bear to read letters such as these I have written to you. It is the weak of soul who will not ask for revelation, because somehow they possess enough Truth by God's grace to know they could not bear to hear the truth regarding how the spiritual really works and what is required of them to progress further into the mysteries of God. But do not look down upon them,

---

* Consider Luke 9:23-26.

for we usually are not given the revelation of where they are on the divine spectrum that is called "God's Satisfaction with the Soul." For God may be very satisfied with what degree of devotion they are willing to give Him given the hardships their soul has had to suffer across its life. Entrust them to God rather than trying to bear a burden of helping them grow if they do not want your help, and God bless you richly for keeping the faith and for diligently pursuing the Truth which is Christ, because this is what your degree of devotion has required of you.

Again, it is no sin to feel misery, but remind your soul with authority that God has made a way out of it. Then get up and start walking away. Treat your misery as a real spiritual entity from which you can walk away. God will guide you and a path will be revealed before you. Whether you are led to step onto the path of quiet gratitude, heartfelt praise, or obedience without feeling—you can trust that He knows which path will get your soul back to the Way of Christ and detached from this misery as quickly as possible.

So please accept that I have the utmost feeling for your state. But accept also if you are able (and I believe you are or you would not have read to the end of this letter), that the best counsel I can give is the exercise of your faith, which includes believing in the spiritual reality that there are rest and renewal in Christ. Lean into the Lord, as John did at that

Supper.* Be humble. Accept with due respect toward God that He most certainly understands your feeling but that He has also made a way out of it.

And peace be with you always.

---

* John 13:23